This Recipe Book Belongs to...

....

....

Table of Contents

Recipe	Page

Table of Contents

Recipe		Page

Table of Contents

Recipe	Page

Table of Contents

Recipe	Page

Recipe ....

Source ....

Ingredients

....

....

....

....

....

....

....

....

....

....

....

This Recipe is Special to our Family because...

....

....

....

....

Directions

Recipe ....

Source ....

Ingredients

....

....

....

....

....

....

....

....

....

....

....

This Recipe is Special to our Family because...

....

....

....

....

Directions

Recipe ....

Source ....

Ingredients

....

....

....

....

....

....

....

....

....

....

....

This Recipe is Special to our Family because...

....

....

....

....

Directions

Recipe ....

Source ....

Ingredients

....

....

....

....

....

....

....

....

....

....

....

....

This Recipe is Special to our Family because...

....

....

....

....

Directions

Recipe ....

Source ....

Ingredients

....

....

....

....

....

....

....

....

....

....

....

....

....

This Recipe is Special to our Family because...

....

....

....

....

Directions

Recipe ....

Source ....

Ingredients

....

....

....

....

....

....

....

....

....

....

....

This Recipe is Special to our Family because...

....

....

....

....

Directions

Recipe ....

Source ....

Ingredients

....

....

....

....

....

....

....

....

....

....

....

This Recipe is Special to our Family because...

....

....

....

....

Directions

Recipe ....

Source ....

Ingredients

....

....

....

....

....

....

....

....

....

....

....

This Recipe is Special to our Family because...

....

....

....

....

Directions

Recipe ....

Source ....

Ingredients

....

....

....

....

....

....

....

....

....

....

....

This Recipe is Special to our Family because...

....

....

....

....

Directions

Recipe ....

Source ....

Ingredients

....

....

....

....

....

....

....

....

....

....

....

This Recipe is Special to our Family because...

....

....

....

....

Directions

Recipe ....

Source ....

Ingredients

....

....

....

....

....

....

....

....

....

....

This Recipe is Special to our Family because...

....

....

....

....

Directions

Recipe ....

Source ....

Ingredients

....

....

....

....

....

....

....

....

....

....

....

....

This Recipe is Special to our Family because...

....

....

....

....

Directions

Recipe ....

Source ....

Ingredients

....

....

....

....

....

....

....

....

....

....

....

This Recipe is Special to our Family because...

....

....

....

....

Directions

Recipe ....

Source ....

Ingredients

....

....

....

....

....

....

....

....

....

....

....

This Recipe is Special to our Family because...

....

....

....

....

Directions

Recipe ....

Source ....

Ingredients

....

....

....

....

....

....

....

....

....

....

....

....

This Recipe is Special to our Family because...

....

....

....

....

Directions

Recipe ....

Source ....

Ingredients

....

....

....

....

....

....

....

....

....

....

....

....

This Recipe is Special to our Family because...

....

....

....

....

Directions

Recipe ....

Source ....

Ingredients

....

....

....

....

....

....

....

....

....

....

....

....

This Recipe is Special to our Family because...

....

....

....

Directions

Recipe ....

Source ....

Ingredients

....

....

....

....

....

....

....

....

....

....

This Recipe is Special to our Family because...

....

....

....

....

Directions

Recipe ....

Source ....

Ingredients

....

....

....

....

....

....

....

....

....

....

This Recipe is Special to our Family because...

....

....

....

....

Directions

Recipe ....

Source ....

Ingredients

....

....

....

....

....

....

....

....

....

....

....

This Recipe is Special to our Family because...

....

....

....

....

Directions

Recipe ....

Source ....

Ingredients

....

....

....

....

....

....

....

....

....

....

....

This Recipe is Special to our Family because...

....

....

....

....

Directions

Recipe ....

Source ....

Ingredients

....

....

....

....

....

....

....

....

....

....

....

....

This Recipe is Special to our Family because...

....

....

....

....

Directions

Recipe ....

Source ....

Ingredients

....

....

....

....

....

....

....

....

....

....

....

This Recipe is Special to our Family because...

....

....

....

....

Directions

Recipe ....

Source ....

Ingredients

....

....

....

....

....

....

....

....

....

....

....

This Recipe is Special to our Family because...

....

....

....

....

Directions

Recipe ....

Source ....

Ingredients

....

....

....

....

....

....

....

....

....

....

....

This Recipe is Special to our Family because...

....

....

....

....

Directions

Recipe ....

Source ....

Ingredients

....

....

....

....

....

....

....

....

....

....

....

This Recipe is Special to our Family because...

....

....

....

....

Directions

Recipe ....

Source ....

Ingredients

....

....

....

....

....

....

....

....

....

....

....

This Recipe is Special to our Family because...

....

....

....

....

Directions

Recipe ....

Source ....

Ingredients

....

....

....

....

....

....

....

....

....

....

....

....

This Recipe is Special to our Family because...

....

....

....

....

Directions

Recipe ....

Source ....

Ingredients

....

....

....

....

....

....

....

....

....

....

....

This Recipe is Special to our Family because...

....

....

....

....

Directions

Recipe ....

Source ....

Ingredients

....

....

....

....

....

....

....

....

....

....

This Recipe is Special to our Family because...

....

....

....

....

Directions

Recipe ....

Source ....

Ingredients

....

....

....

....

....

....

....

....

....

....

....

....

This Recipe is Special to our Family because...

....

....

....

....

Directions

Recipe ....

Source ....

Ingredients

....

....

....

....

....

....

....

....

....

....

....

This Recipe is Special to our Family because...

....

....

....

....

Directions

Recipe ....

Source ....

Ingredients

....

....

....

....

....

....

....

....

....

....

....

This Recipe is Special to our Family because...

....

....

....

....

Directions

Recipe ....

Source ....

Ingredients

....

....

....

....

....

....

....

....

....

....

....

....

This Recipe is Special to our Family because...

....

....

....

....

Directions

Recipe ....

Source ....

Ingredients

....

....

....

....

....

....

....

....

....

....

....

This Recipe is Special to our Family because...

....

....

....

....

Directions

Recipe ....

Source ....

Ingredients

....

....

....

....

....

....

....

....

....

....

This Recipe is Special to our Family because...

....

....

....

....

Directions

Recipe ....

Source ....

Ingredients

....

....

....

....

....

....

....

....

....

....

....

This Recipe is Special to our Family because...

....

....

....

....

Directions

Recipe ....

Source ....

Ingredients

....

....

....

....

....

....

....

....

....

....

....

This Recipe is Special to our Family because...

....

....

....

....

Directions

Recipe ....

Source ....

Ingredients

....

....

....

....

....

....

....

....

....

....

....

....

This Recipe is Special to our Family because...

....

....

....

....

Directions

Recipe ....

Source ....

Ingredients

....

....

....

....

....

....

....

....

....

....

....

This Recipe is Special to our Family because...

....

....

....

....

Directions

Recipe ....

Source ....

Ingredients

....

....

....

....

....

....

....

....

....

....

This Recipe is Special to our Family because...

....

....

....

....

Directions

Recipe ....

Source ....

Ingredients

....

....

....

....

....

....

....

....

....

....

This Recipe is Special to our Family because...

....

....

....

....

Directions

Recipe ....

Source ....

Ingredients

....

....

....

....

....

....

....

....

....

....

....

This Recipe is Special to our Family because...

....

....

....

....

Directions

Recipe ....

Source ....

Ingredients

....

....

....

....

....

....

....

....

....

....

....

This Recipe is Special to our Family because...

....

....

....

....

Directions

Recipe ....

Source ....

Ingredients

....

....

....

....

....

....

....

....

....

....

....

This Recipe is Special to our Family because...

....

....

....

....

Directions

Recipe ....

Source ....

Ingredients

....

....

....

....

....

....

....

....

....

....

....

This Recipe is Special to our Family because...

....

....

....

....

Directions

Recipe ....

Source ....

Ingredients

....

....

....

....

....

....

....

....

....

....

This Recipe is Special to our Family because...

....

....

....

....

Directions

Recipe ....

Source ....

Ingredients

....

....

....

....

....

....

....

....

....

....

This Recipe is Special to our Family because...

....

....

....

....

Directions

Recipe ....

Source ....

Ingredients

....

....

....

....

....

....

....

....

....

....

This Recipe is Special to our Family because...

....

....

....

....

Directions

Recipe ....

Source ....

Ingredients

This Recipe is Special to our Family because...

Directions

Recipe ....

Source ....

Ingredients

....

....

....

....

....

....

....

....

....

....

This Recipe is Special to our Family because...

....

....

....

....

Directions

Recipe ....

Source ....

Ingredients

....

....

....

....

....

....

....

....

....

....

....

....

This Recipe is Special to our Family because...

....

....

....

....

Directions

Published in 2017 by
Tri-Moon Press

Printed in the United States of America

Made in the USA
San Bernardino, CA
05 March 2019